Introduction To Devops Learn Devops Basics In 60 Minutes

SADANAND PUJARI

Published by SADANAND PUJARI, 2023.

Table of Contents

Copyright

Introduction To Devops Learn Devops Basics In 60 Minutes

First Edition: Dec 2023

Book Design by **SADANAND PUJARI**

About

Do you need to understand the basics of DevOps? Have you found that many training resources use complex technical jargon that makes it difficult to understand the basic concepts? If you need to get a basic understanding of DevOps quickly and clearly, this is the Book for you.

If you need the basics of DevOps, this Book will give you a strong foundation, and is the ideal starting point.

If you are a project manager, developer, or operations administrator who needs a basic understanding of DevOps, this is the Book for you!

Introduction to DevOps

Hello. Welcome to the DevOps Foundation Book. Upon successful completion of this Book, you will be able to articulate the benefits of implementing the Full Stack of DevOps: culture practices and automation at your organization to achieve the ultimate goal of improving quality, increasing speed and reducing costs of IT services. By the end of this Book, you will be able to explain the basic concepts, principles and scope of DevOps, including The Three Ways and accelerator's, such as Lean and Agile that supports the evolution and emergence of the DevOps movement.

You will be able to summarize the cultural, structural and technological barriers that IT faces when attempting to deliver services at the right quality, speed and cost, and why challenges are faced when implementing DevOps in today's organizations. We'll also discuss 15 very specific practices related to culture, processes and automation that are must-haves for effective delivery of DevOps. You will also be able to describe how DevOps practices transform processes, utilizing Lean, Agile, and ITSM accelerators to solve the process design problems facing IT.

Here you can see the Book structure. Now, we are on the very first chapter, which is the introduction to DevOps. Most IT professionals have heard or read about DevOps. Some of them know what DevOps is, whereas others have a limited understanding or misperceptions about DevOps. To help you understand DevOps comprehensively, this chapter not only defines DevOps, but also explains DevOps as a "Full Stack" of culture, practices and automation.

At the end of this chapter, you will be able to describe what DevOps is, and what it is not. You will also be able to explain the approach of thinking about the critical success factors of DevOps as a Full Stack of culture, practices, and automation and determining what it means for your organization.

What is Devops

DevOps is used to describe an evolution of existing IT best practices from ITIL, Lean and Agile into a development and operations approach that supports automation and continuous delivery. DevOps encourages a culture of collaboration and learning to help IT deliver business value better, faster, and cheaper than ever before. In this chapter, we will look at what DevOps is. DevOps is a movement, philosophy or ideology.

DevOps is about the relationship between Development and Operations. It encourages IT operations to interact with Development differently, and vice versa. DevOps is designed to shift and permeate throughout the entire culture of an organization. DevOps is about communication and collaboration. It uses automation and new tools to enable better communication and collaboration. DevOps is about Development and Operations. It focuses on culture, automation and new practices, which can be used to address the challenges of diverse organizations. DevOps is about balancing speed and change with Development, with the reliability and stability required by Operations. DevOps is flexible enough to be workable, even in regulated environments. In this chapter, we will look at what DevOps is not.

DevOps is not a specific job, title or team. DevOps is not only for startups or web applications. It is a movement of principles, practices and values. DevOps is not designed to replace Operations. Instead, it is meant to encourage collaboration between Development and Operations. DevOps is not only about tools or automation. While there may not be an alternative way to state exactly what DevOps is, certain concepts and ideas help us understand it. One important concept is the Full Stack. The Full Stack approach helps decision makers to look at DevOps and their organizations holistically and gives them the widest view of what DevOps can do for diverse organizations. The core aspects of the Full Stack approach includes the important concept you learned when you reviewed the definition of DevOps.

The full stack represents the three core aspects of any DevOps implementation that represent critical factors for success by creating the right culture with the right people. putting the right processes and practices into place, and adding the level of technology and automation to that culture and those practices to streamline and accelerate them. While the Full Stack approach is not meant to be prescriptive, thinking about DevOps in this way gives business an idea of not only the scope of the changes that decision makers may wish to implement, but also the scope of the benefits and rewards.

Business Value

We finished the introductory model of this Book. And now we are on the first model, which is the Business value of DevOps. In this chapter, you will learn about business value, dimensions of business value, customer value hierarchy, external drivers of change, goals of DevOps, Systems Thinking, digital disruption, IT downward spiral, technical debt and so on. Finally, you will understand how DevOps helps IT find the balance between speed and quality.

At the end of this chapter, you will be able to explain the need for DevOps as a solution to problems facing organizations today. And summarize how the need for more value from IT drives the business toward DevOps. In this chapter, we will try to answer the following question. What is business value? Business value is the level to which a service meets customer's expectations or exceeds them. The service has customers at its core. A business creates value through services and sets expectations in response to the requirements of its customers. For customers, any business creates value when it achieves its own stated objectives and keeps its promises. You have learned about business value and how it is created. One way to think about business value is to consider it as reflecting three dimensions.

The three dimensions of business value are quality, cost and speed. The first dimension is service quality - the customer's specific or functional requirements and (non-functional) warranty. The second dimension is the cost. Businesses operate at a cost. This cost is often measured against how much customers are willing to pay. In other words, the customer's perceived value. Services need to be affordable to the customers and profitable for the business. Increasingly, businesses also need to operate at a required speed. It is fine if businesses are delivering quality. But what if they're delivering it a day later to the scheduled date? Speed is particularly relevant to the business problem in the present context, because customer expectations around it have changed immensely in recent years. Businesses should focus on balancing the three dimensions. It is not enough to only be concerned with or balance one or two out of the three dimensions. Remember the dimensions, we all have different priorities for diverse customers at various points in their lifecycle.

Quality may matter more to a customer who is financially stable or when the economy is good. Cost may be a crucial dimension during an economic recession, or the customer who is dealing with financial issues. Many businesses are under pressure to provide value at the same levels of quality and cost to customers but at an accelerated speed, which results in increased pressure on IT to deliver. In 1984, Professor Noriaki Kano developed a customer satisfaction model referred to as the Kano Model that classified customer preferences into several categories. Understanding the customer value attributes helps us understand why IT is increasingly being asked by their business to deliver better, faster and cheaper results to achieve business value. The three customer value attributes are: Basic attributes, Performance attributes and Excitement attributes. These attributes are not static as customer expectations change. Features that customers value and expect drift over time, and features once considered differentiators and exciters to customers eventually become expected, boring and even dissatisfying without continued innovation.

The first attribute is the basic attributes. They must have features that are essential requirements customers expect and take for granted. These attributes generally do not create value in and of themselves, but they are simply what businesses need to enter the market. Without them, customers will be highly dissatisfied. The second one is Performance attributes. They are Want to Have features that drive customer dissatisfaction. If done well, they allow businesses to compete with others. And conversely, their absence may cause dissatisfaction. As a general rule, competing organizations offer Performance attributes to varying degrees of quality. Finally, there are attributes that really differentiate businesses in the market and make customers say WOW.

These attributes drive customer satisfaction, but because they are innovative or new to customers, they do not result in dissatisfaction if they are not present. Continuing to offer those exciting attributes requires constant innovation, improvement and research to stay ahead of the curve. When learning about the definition of business value, you learned that customer expectations change, and the category of the Kano model in which an attribute belongs drifts over time. A service, product or feature that is innovative today becomes a standard offering over time because of customer demand. Customer requirements and expectations have changed significantly in the last three years, moving at an increasingly rapid pace.

In response, organizations of all kinds have become progressively more reliant on IT to directly deliver business value to the end customer. Now, more than ever before, IT must deliver more value at a faster pace through services that are of higher quality and produced at lower costs. And these demands are increasing almost exponentially. Companies live and die on their ability to discover new businesses and create ongoing value for customers. This has always been true, but never more so than in the past few years. Competitive pressure is increasing, fueled by rapid changes in technology and society.

External Drivers of Change

Because of external drivers of change, we have seen rapid changes in technology and society. The four important drivers are The Emergence of Cloud Technology. Global Supply, Workforce Automation and Digitally Disruptive Competition. The emergence of cloud technology. The emergence of cloud technology has had an enormous impact on IT. Cloud technology contributes to the increasing demand from business partners, stakeholders and customers. The demands are regarding speed, flexibility and innovation.

In Nicolas Carr's book, The Big Switch, he states that cloud technology will transform the industry in a way electrical distribution networks transformed the world at the end of the 19th century. That is how enormous the impact of cloud technology both is and potentially could be as a disruptive force in the world. In recent years, the availability of high-capacity networks, low-cost computers, and storage and other factors have led to the growth in cloud computing. It has also led to cheaper service costs. Further, the emergence of cloud technology has allowed businesses to avoid or minimize their upfront IT infrastructure costs and get applications up and running faster. Therefore, organizations are under increasing pressure to lower their IT infrastructure costs to remain competitive.

Global supply. Thomas Friedman in his book The World is Flat, analyzes the impact of globalization. The title alludes to the idea that there is a shift in perception required for countries, companies and individuals to remain competitive in a marketplace, which is increasingly global and where historical and geographic divisions are becoming irrelevant. With global boundaries becoming increasingly meaningless, the race to be the best, the fastest, the cheapest has intensified. In addition, more and more businesses are driven to expand globally. They are increasingly reliant on technology to enable global expansion. Workforce automation. An industry trend is to fully automate repetitive work.

Workforce automation is changing how businesses think about traditional IT operations, monitoring and IT management work such as running batch jobs, backing up IT systems, and deploying changes to production systems. While these tasks have been done manually in the past, they are rapidly moving toward automation as a means of achieving improved quality, speed, cost, and the ability to quickly fall back to a book and recover previous versions. To be effective, automation demands a supportive culture and practices. Digitally disruptive competition. The impact of the first three drivers on the speed at which an existing or new competitor is able to enter a market and put pressure on brick and mortar business models results in digitally disruptive competition.

While competition has always been a reality, what is new is the ubiquitous availability of cloud based technical services and offshoring options available at seemingly low costs and faster speeds compared to traditional delivery models. The lease versus buy cloud services model has leveled the playing field and enabled business competition to rapidly come to market and disrupt traditional commercial models without having made years of investment in data centers, software factories or network infrastructure.

Newly formed, built-on-the-web, app-enabled brands are now able to leverage cloud based services and software as a service business automation for core business processes in a matter of weeks, if not days. They are highly enabled. Further, they enter a market with new and disruptive products in a fraction of the time it would take for a traditional brick and mortar organization to respond. Cloud has indeed changed everything! The truth of this trend has given rise to the popular phrase "digital transformation". This digital transformation is accelerating the pace of the changing customer expectations and creating a movement that is redefining how we achieve customer value.

Silo Mentality

Now review the organizational goals of DevOps. These goals are neither you nor were they created by the DevOps movement. Yet, their successful execution has eluded most IT organizations for decades. Most importantly, IT organizations have had the means, frameworks, tools and prescriptive guidance to achieve them, but they have failed to use and apply them in an integrated manner. So, what is different now that has not been the case for the last 20 years?

Why do we think that this new "DevOps movement" will achieve success where many of the frameworks have come and gone without invoking meaningful change? DevOps seeks to facilitate digital transformation. Digital transformation allows businesses to leverage the changes and opportunities that are presented by digital technologies. It also allows them to benefit from their accelerating impact in a strategic and prioritized way so that the technologies become a strategic advantage and not a roadblock or challenge to be overcome.

From the perspective of the overall business, digital transformation is a requirement and an urgent necessity. However, as you have learned, facilitating that transformation means removing the disconnect between different factors within IT Development and Operations. as well as between internal business partners or stakeholders and IT so that real value can be achieved. From the IT perspective, while the need for digital transformation is often understood, it seems impossible to facilitate in the current environment. So why is that? Now that you understand the reasons for the increased demand from IT to deliver better, faster and cheaper results and, ultimately increase business value, what are the barriers to delivering that value?

Review the IT value delivery problem to learn about the barriers in the next chapter. You will first review the big cultural challenge that IT often faces when asked to deliver business value. This challenge is the organizational structure of both the business and IT, which is simply not created for today's requirements. You will also understand that the organizational structure has its roots in the long past. In the 1700s, Adam Smith, the influential author of The Wealth of Nations, believed and taught that the best way to take an unskilled workforce and have them produce a quality product consistently was to artificially break a process apart into the smallest repeatable task and have that task performed repeatedly by the same resource.

Management emphasized the importance of this model of task specialization, so it was further refined throughout the Industrial Revolution. In the 20th century, it informed the concept of Fordism named for Henry Ford. In 1908, he revolutionized American industry with the Ford Model T, which provided a model for mass production driven by the assembly line. In 1911, Frederick Taylor took Smith and Ford's notions further and introduced the concept of "scientific management", one of the earliest management ideas to reach a mass audience. It promoted applying the scientific method to organizational structure - using precise measurements and data to set specific, high productivity targets for workers to achieve - and it became very popular throughout corporate America.

These ideas are still with us to this day - functionality, they are responsible for establishing the management levels within organizational hierarchies that are considered necessary to oversee the activities of these single tasked workers or specialist groups. Well into the 21st century, organizations continue to emphasize task specialization, control and measurement within their cultures and environments. You have learned how silos became the norm. Now, before we move forward, review the meaning of the silo mentality.

A silo mentality occurs when a team or department shares a set of common tasks, but operates distinctly from other groups with their power derived from association with a function or shared technical knowledge. In the heavily siloed organization, cooperation, collaboration and communication are reduced, and roles and departments are not designed to be cross-functional. Each individual or functional team views their objectives only through the lens of the individual tasks and responsibilities, especially those specific tasks that they are measured against. They lack the proper incentives or resources to respond to the needs of other teams or the departments, or to the needs of the business. as a whole. Silo mentality leads to a lack of Systems Thinking and creates that Wall of Confusion between Development and Operations.

It is important to understand the impact of a lack of Systems Thinking and the Wall of Confusion on IT's ability to deliver business value. It is also important to understand how our organizational cultures and hierarchies have evolved over time and created today's cultural challenge of a silo mentality. Systems Thinking means understanding that that single business function is an interrelated, interdependent part of a larger system. The slogan "Think globally, act locally" is a good example. The environment is deteriorating on a global basis, so we recycle our aluminum and plastic locally. When you view yourself as only existing in your team or area, there is limited focus placed on a sense of collective responsibility.

In the business enterprise, there is also a limited focus of value placed on your role in the larger organization - on the work that is assigned to you and on the results and the impact of the work once it is assigned to someone else for further processing. Organizational silos that lack Systems Thinking as the equivalent of trying to get where you need to be without a map. You are orienting yourself toward goals without knowing why or what the result of each measurement and each objective completed will be, or how it will affect the organization as a whole.

The incentives that cause a silo mentality and the lack of Systems Thinking distort your sense of accountability. The Wall of Confusion is a scenario in which Development and Operations don't fundamentally understand why the other side does things the way that they do, or what their needs are, which degrades their ability to come together to deliver business value. In almost every organization, the development and operations teams operate in separate silos, and they are accountable for and measured against competing sets of priorities and concerns. They are expected to simultaneously pursue two very different goals that include responding to rapid changes that take place in customer and business expectations to remain competitive. Or, providing customers and the business with a stable, reliable and secure infrastructure.

18

Development is more focused on agility, new technologies and speed to achieve the first goal, while Operations is more concerned with maturity, compliance and risk management to achieve the second. This really puts Development and Operations in a position where the best possible outcome will be achieved if Development and Operations work together toward a common goal. But if they cannot work together because their respective goals are often directly in opposition with each other.

Local Optimization and Bureaucracy

Without Systems Thinking or a sense of accountability to the large organization and its goals, each silo will optimize its processes locally within their limited worldview. Local optimization produces the best results for an individual or a team. While it is important to create local efficiencies, businesses need to understand that process design that is locally optimized within a silo can potentially create a situation that limits value realization.

Locally optimized processes, practices and solutions mean that work may get done within each individual area, but challenges arise with prioritization and productivity when there is a handoff between groups. This often results in units of work being placed in a non-active waiting state where nothing moves forward. It also means that there is more attention paid to the benefits of shared capabilities and resources, and instead, they are recreated or duplicated within each area. This lack of attention then generates a high likelihood of redundant processes and resources and encourages non-integrated solutions. Silos lead to local optimization and poor overall process design at the organizational level.

The organizational structure that creates silos also encourages the silo mentality. Silos are often created in response to bureaucracy. Bureaucracy can have a negative impact on the processes and practices of IT and add levels of complexity, redundancy and inefficiency that are functionally unnecessary. While bureaucracy can be necessary to achieve common goals and does have many positive effects, the problem arises when it is not fit-for-purpose and begins to impose constraints and limitations on the ability of the functional areas to deliver overall value. Therefore, it is important to understand the strengths and weaknesses of bureaucracy. The end result of silos that are locally optimized but are not integrated or able to collaborate is waste. Businesses should evaluate wasted time, energy, effort and resources, as well as aspects of processes that get in the way and are unnecessary.

Review examples of waste created because of processes that are overly complex, bureaucratic, and inefficient, and that act as barriers to IT being able to deliver business value. Recurrent incidents that occur hundreds of times without anyone looking at the root cause of the problem. It assets that are poorly tracked, controlled or inventoried. Multiple service desks all with their own tools and separate processes. Redundant or duplicate tools purchased by various IT departments in the same organization.

Supplier contracts that expire without knowledge until an incident occurs. Incident tickets that disappear into an IT back office black hole until someone brings them to everyone's notice. Massive amounts of wasted server capacity due to a lack of capacity and demand management. And multiple change management processes due to political boundaries.

Big Shift

The result of all the waste and the complexity and redundancy in processes is that in recent years, IT has been simply unable to grow and transform itself in the way that the business requires, since it is too busy keeping its head above the water. As a result, the percentage of budget spent on maintaining the business has also grown while the capacity for innovation has decreased. The challenges that exist in processes and practices have carried over into the technology and tools IT uses.

Because IT lacks the capacity and resources to innovate, grow or transform, they often find themselves without the time to move to new tools and by necessity, fall back on the legacy tools because the existing process won't support anything else. The silo mentality and local optimization also discourages integration and the sharing of tools across teams, resulting in an organization where teams that use the same tools do not use them in the same way or in ways that are most efficient. Without integration, true automation becomes impossible. And many processors that could be automated continue to be manual. These elements result in a reliance on systems and tools that over time become propped up and function only with a patchwork of short-term fixes and unfulfilled intentions to "fix things later". In this chapter, review the concept of IT Downward Spiral that leads into an explanation of technical debt.

The downward spiral occurs in three stages. Step one: Operations inherits a challenge. In the first stage, IT Operations encounters applications and infrastructure in their daily work that are overly complex, not documented properly, fragile, and prone to failure. Under pressure to maintain stability for customers, they don't have time to address the root cause of the issue. And even if they did, they may not have access to or be aware of how to communicate these issues to Development or the necessary people in the organization. Because of this issue, they see failure at some point. Step two: Development is pressure to Fix it Fast.

When a failure occurs, things move to the second stage where someone - a product manager or someone at the top of the organization - attempts to compensate for the failure by promising a bigger, bolder Book correction, oblivious to what the technology can or cannot support. Development is asked to solve these new technical challenges quickly, and they are forced to cut corners in order to meet an unrealistic deadline. They rush to fix the issues and tell themselves that they will return to the project later to make improvements or updates, but they never have time to come back to it. Step three: Operations includes a new set of challenges.

Finally, a rushed, potentially flawed solution to the problem is implemented, which then brings its own challenges to Operations and leads back to the first stage all over again. Technical debt accumulates in much the same way that monetary debt does. When the cost of rework and overly complex business demands time from those in Operations, it decreases their ability to address previous failures or provide feedback to Development. As a result, Development is expected to compensate for those failures.

The true result of technical debt is a reduction in business value delivered. Because of less time to address past releases that will be flawed and so on, the Development team is unable to fix the issue holistically. Their situation is similar to the one in which interest on monetary debt decreases your ability to pay the original debt back. Once that happens, things only get worse because production cycles get slower and slower. People get less and less ambitious about undertaking new projects and few new projects are completed.

DevOps to Find the Balance

What happens if IT can't deliver value? As the internal and external demand for IT services increases, IT faces a corresponding decrease in their own capabilities for the reasons described earlier in this Book. The culture of silos that lack Systems Thinking causes local optimization. Bureaucracy adds additional complexity to the problem and results in poorly designed processes and practices with a lot of waste. As a result, IT must spend a larger share of their time and effort on keeping the business running, leaving them with limited time to grow or innovate.

Over time, the systems and tools they use become overburdened with technical debt. All these issues ultimately feed into each other in a vicious downward spiral that continues to get worse and leaves IT unable to deliver the value that is demanded and required from them. DevOps seeks to solve all these issues. This isn't just a problem for stake stakeholders and management within an organization. This problem isn't just because internal partners and stakeholders demand too much or do not provide adequate support to IT to do what is being asked of them. It is a cultural, practical and technological problem. It is a value gap that we must address.

The decision to pursue DevOps is for many IT shops, a decision that could affect their very existence. If it isn't addressed, then organizational leadership will make decisions that it will not like. And it is already starting to happen in many organizations. The growth of cloud technology and global supply options that are driving the increased demand from customers, partners and stakeholders also means that IT is seeing increased competition. Organizations have more options that are available to them if they decide to seek alternative IT options. There is an observable trend towards that usage of "shadow IT" investments - situations where a line of business produces their IT services directly from the external market or funds their own IT capability due to the perception of poor quality, slow speed or higher cost of existing options.

"Shadow IT" is just another way of saying "loss of market share for internal IT". If this goes on long enough and an organization loses the funding it requests based on expected revenue, then there is the only one possible financial outcome. At a more micro level, the goals of IT are not dissimilar from those of the larger organization when it comes to what the DevOps needs to address. Reviews the goals of DevOps. Faster delivery of features. Customers, internal partners and stakeholders demand faster time to market, which means IT needs to deliver features faster than they usually do. Continuous software delivery. The ultimate goal of IT is to provide the value that is demanded and required of them. Increased collaboration and communication. Internal partners and stakeholders need that integration with IT, which means that IT requires increased collaboration and communication internally to both itself and the organization as a whole.

More productive teams. Internal partners and stakeholders need increased productivity, which IT can support through teams that are more productive. More time to innovate. Customers, internal partners and stakeholders also need increased flexibility and agility, which IT can provide if it has more time to innovate. Faster resolution of problems. Internal partners and stakeholders need improved responsiveness from IT, which means IT requires a way to provide faster resolution of problems. Reduced complexity to manage. Internal partners and stakeholders are demanding better visibility and transparency, which IT can achieve through processes that have a reduced complexity to manage.

DevOps helps IT find the balance. Remember the wall of confusion between Development and Operations - a place where Development and Operations met with opposing priorities? DevOps has emerged to help IT find the balance and achieves the seemingly impossible goal of integration around the singular focus of delivering business value. Today's organizations increasingly require both stability and change at the same time while maintaining an unprecedented level of quality.

CALMS

We finished the first chapter of this Book. And now we are on the second chapter, which is the key DevOps principles and concepts. In this chapter, you will discover the key principles and concepts of DevOps. You will also review the meaning of the acronym CALMS and understand its significance as the key pillars and concepts that underpin DevOps. Further, you will learn about the importance of The Three Ways and the scope of the Full Stack.

At the end of this chapter, you will be able to explain the basic concepts, principles, and scope of DevOps, including the Three ways and accelerators, such as Lean and Agile that supports evolution and emergence of the DevOps movement and summarize the cultural, structural and technological barriers that IT faces when attempting to deliver services at the right quality, speed and cost. And why challenges are faced when implementing DevOps in today's organizations.

CALMS is an acronym originally developed by John Willis and Damon Edwards in 2010. Juz Humble refined it to facilitate a better understanding of the key pillars and concepts that underpin DevOps, namely culture, automation, lean, measurement and sharing. CALMS is critical and central to DevOps implementation. CALMS stands for Culture, Automation, Lean, Measurement and Sharing.

The First Way: Flow

The objective of the First Way is to identify how individual pieces fit together, understand what things are moving from team to team, why they are moving, and what steps will be all the way to delivery of the product to the customer. The First Way focuses on understanding how work flows, how work moves from Development to Operations, and then from the functional areas of the business to customers - from left to right, one team to another.

Flow is about identifying the constraints discussed earlier. Understanding where the bottlenecks are and where productivity is slowest so that you can then prioritize the improvements for the biggest impact. When you understand how the work flows, you can clearly identify obstacles contributing to that Wall of Confusion and eliminate them. Over time, processes may become slow, inefficient and needlessly complex. When this happens, they impose additional challenges and slow things down even further because bottlenecks occur. In his 1984 novel, The Goal, Dr. Eliahu Goldratt introduced the Theory of Constraints.

This theory states that no complex system or process can be more efficient or stronger than its most limiting bottleneck or constraint. To state it differently, no process or flow of work can go any faster than its slowest step. The theory helps organizations identify and focus on the one area that is the slowest and most inefficient because that area constrains the entire system. When organizations apply the theory and address the issues, they increase the speed of progress for the entire system. Earlier, you learned about flow as the First Way of DevOps. Flow ideally means that work moves from person to person, from team to team, along the value stream, unconstrained at the high velocity. Lean values and Lean processes focus on constraints and on the concept of flow.

How work moves across silos and teams from beginning to end, and how to streamline, simplify and get everyone working at the same speed. One of the key tools available in Lean is value stream mapping. It means constantly measuring performance, using the data to focus on particular problem areas or determine where the waste is occurring and why it is happening. Leaders can then apply the appropriate improvements to the flow of work. You will now learn how to increase the flow of the work. The focus is on a variety of cultural changes, new processes or practices, and technology and automation approaches designed to increase flow. Review further to understand some practices that increase flow. Increase transparency and visibility of work. In IT, work is often invisible, because unlike manufacturing, inventory and production do not involve physical goods. It is easier for work to pile up or impede the flow without anyone realizing it or seeing its impact.

DevOps practices like visual management allow us to focus on these areas and make the invisible visible. Place limits on work in progress. IT is very dynamic. Because of constant inputs and multiple stakeholders demanding different priority outputs at the same time. IT professionals are often multitasking, distracted and sometimes overwhelmed. Work in progress limits speak to this issue by introducing the concept of work capacity into IT.

Work in smaller batches. A more iterative approach to development with Agile practices, such as Scrum allows teams to catch defects and errors early on their work and reduces rework and waste. Reduce the number of handoffs. Every time what passes from one person to another, or from one team to the other, there is a significant amount of communication involved.

Wait times in between these handoffs act as a constraint and slow down the flow of work. Inevitably, knowledge is also lost during these handoffs. DevOps strives to reduce the number of handoffs, and its approach to structure and teaming increases accountability and self-management. Identify and prioritize constraints or bottlenecks. A system's speed is generally set by its slowest point. DevOps provides tools to help identify and prioritize constraints to make the biggest impact.

Eliminate waste wherever possible. DevOps was built on Lean and Agile, and the elimination of waste is its central focus. DevOps constantly strives to improve so that it can eliminate waste wherever possible.

The Second Way: Feedback

While the First Way describes the principles that enable the fast flow of work from left to right, The Second Way describes the principles that enable the reciprocal, that is, fast and constant feedback from right to left in all the stages of the value stream. The Second Way emphasizes communication and collaboration, which are required to improve the product. The Second Way is about strengthening and automating feedback loops, closing them to promote consistency and regularity of communication, and ensuring that feedback gives rise to meaningful action and change. Feedback loops need to be fast and accurate. They need to connect to Development and Operations and to all stakeholders.

The Second Way helps to create safer and more resilient systems of work because it provides more opportunities to detect and correct errors. DevOps encourages a cultural shift, new processes and practices, and new approaches to technology and automation to support feedback loops and increase quality and resiliency. Review further to understand the ways through which DevOps increases quality and resiliency. Detect problems as they occur. DevOps practices such as Scrum and Visual Management offer opportunities to provide quick feedback.

The DevOps approach to measurement also ensures that problems are detected as they occur and not later in the workflow. Swarm to solve problems and gain new knowledge. In a workflow, detecting problems does not end the problem. Teams must also respond to them. This step involves being able to collaborate quickly, to swarm, and to use problem solving opportunities as a learning opportunity to gain new knowledge and ensure that solutions are disseminated as widely as possible. Push quality closer to the source. DevOps structures and teaming are about increasing accountability and reducing handoffs to keep the quality closer to where the work is performed.

The more checks that are in place and the more people or teams the work must move through, the more likely it is that knowledge will degrade and that errors will occur with each handoff. Optimize globally versus locally. DevOps encourages Systems Thinking, and seeing the larger picture enables you to take accountability for where your work fits in globally. You may identify a local improvement, which would help only you and your silo. Applying Systems Thinking, you would consider whether the local improvement implemented globally would benefit the entire organization. As shared earlier, DevOps encourages a cultural shift, new processes and practices, and new approaches to technology and automation to support building a culture of experimentation and continual learning. You will now learn the ways to which DevOps can encourage experimentation and continual learning.

Enable a safe culture for learning. In an organizational culture, it is quite common for IT individuals to feel that they will be penalized for sharing problems, suppressed if they make suggestions or blamed for failure. A safe culture for learning sees failure as an opportunity to gain knowledge and does not focus on blame or punishment when problems occur. Institutionalize Continuous Daily Improvement. When daily maintenance and "keeping the lights on " become the priority, It leaves no time for continual improvement or innovation. A DevOps culture is one that ensures continuous improvement is a daily priority, and the processes and practices and focuses on automation are about creating the time to do just that. Turn local knowledge into global improvements.

Local optimization does not always have to be negative, and in cases where local knowledge exists, DevOps encourages teams and individuals to share it for the benefit of everyone in the organization. Implement resilience patterns in daily work. DevOps encourages the implementation of resilience patterns, that is, ways to anticipate problems and ensure that one is prepared and ready to handle them when they arise. Transform leadership to encourage learning. Transformational leadership is a key driver of cultural change. DevOps focuses on ensuring that leaders within organizations support a culture that encourages learning.

The Third Way: Continual Experimentation

The Third Way focuses on creating a culture of continuous experimentation and learning - to enable the ongoing creation of knowledge for individuals, teams and the entire organization.

The Third Way involves breaking down the silo culture. Silo culture often becomes a culture of fear and low trust. The third way helps IT to embrace failure as a learning experience and to view failure as necessary for innovation.

Continuous Delivery Across the Deployment Pipeline

A continuous delivery pipeline is an implementation of the continuous paradigm, where automated builds, tests and deployments are orchestrated as one release workflow. Put more plainly, a CD pipeline is a set of steps your code changes will go through to make their way to production. A CD pipeline delivers, as per business needs, quality products frequently and predictably from test to staging to production in an automated fashion.

Continuous integration is a practice of automating the integration of code changes from multiple contributors into a single software project. It's a primary DevOps best practice, allowing developers to frequently merge code changes into a central repository where builds and tests then run. Automated tools are used to assert the new code's correctness before integration. A source code version control system is the crux of the CI process. The version control system is also supplemented with other checks like automated code quality tests, syntax style review tools, and more. Continuous testing in DevOps is a type of software testing that involves testing at every stage of the development lifecycle.

The goal of continuous testing is to evaluate the quality of the software as part of a continuous delivery process, by testing early and often. You can see the different types of tests at different stages of the development lifecycle in this chapter. Continuous deployment is the continuation of continuous integration. Once the tests have been validated on the development environment, it must be put into production. Continuous deployment, therefore, consists of automating deployment actions that were previously performed manually. In this chapter, we will look at the difference between the functional testing and non-functional testing, Functional testing is a type of testing which verifies that each function of the software application operates in conformance with the requirement specification.

This testing mainly involves black box testing, and it is not concerned about the source code of the application. It is testing those features that are necessary for the product to work. Non-functional testing is defined as a type of software testing to check non-functional aspects or testing of system operations. For example, performance, security, compliance, capacity, and reliability and others. In this chapter, you can review the benefits of continuous delivery.

The components and practices of the deployment pipeline produce continuous delivery, address the IT value delivery problem, and help IT to deliver business value. The practices that enable continuous delivery have their roots in Lean, Agile and ITSM. You can see that effective test data management leads to less rework. Comprehensive, fast and reliable test and deployment automation leads to lower levels of deployment pain.

Trunk based development and continuous integration leads to higher levels of IT performance. Application code, app and system configuration all in version control leads to lower change failure rates. And incorporating security into the delivery process leads to stronger identification with the organization you work for.

The Full Stack

Now, review the scope of DevOps along the lines of the Full Stack. The value delivery problem in IT is that changes are required not just to one area. For example, only to culture, processes or technology. But to every aspect of the full stack. The challenges that IT face today demand that businesses enable the Three Ways and achieve continuous delivery across the deployment pipeline. This approach requires a cultural shift, a new set of practices, and the ability to reach a high maturity level around tools and automation.

DevOps builds on existing practices of ITIL, Lean and Agile. However, none of these frameworks or approaches have been effective historically because they are not implemented with a scope of DevOps. DevOps uses the Full Stack approach to transform people and culture, process and practices, technology and automation. The Full Stack includes a layer that addresses challenges related to people and culture. It focuses on the barriers that currently exist within IT to break down silos and a Wall of Confusion, which encourages a culture of communication, collaboration and experimentation.

One of the biggest barriers to cultural shift is leadership. DevOps addresses the need for transformational leadership and advocates for new approaches to structures and teams within IT hence removing the silo mentality and facilitating the necessary cultural transformation. The second layer of the Full Stack addresses challenges related to processes and practices. In this chapter, you can see the 15 practices of DevOps, which we will go through in the next chapters. This layer ensures that with the right culture in place, processes by default become simplified and streamlined. It builds on the principles of Lean with a focus on problem solving and utilizing tools such as Kaizen process improvement and visual management.

DevOps builts on Agile development and product management ideas, incorporating Scrum practices, the Scaled Agile Frameworks and Agile XP. It incorporates aspects of IT service management and ITIL. DevOps takes all of these existing practices and concepts and uses them to achieve the Three Ways and to enable continuous delivery. The third and the upper layer of the Full Stack addresses challenges related to technology, how to take the right processes and practices and speed them up through integration and automation.

This approach involves integrated toolchains, understanding which tools to use and how to integrate them across teams to enable automation of a variety of processes. DevOps involves developing a high sophistication and maturity level related to automation of the development pipeline. Finally, it involves an understanding of how to leverage cloud technology and virtualization to further speed things up and increase collaboration and efficiency.

Structure

In this chapter, you will understand the culture that supports DevOps. You will also review the significance of collaboration and sharing, key characteristics of collaboration, importance of transformational leadership, characteristics of a transformational leader, DevOps structure and teaming, and the organizational models that support successful implementation of DevOps.

At the end of this chapter, you will be able to summarize the cultural, structural and technological barriers that IT faces when attempting to deliver a service at the right quality, speed and cost, and why challenges are faced with implementing DevOps in today's organizations. We will list the ways in which DevOps transforms culture and better organizes people to solve the cultural and structural challenges facing IT and explain the way that DevOps structures teams and people within an organization in support of its culture, processes, and technologies.

Culture

Culture is learned within an organization. It takes its cue from observable patterns of behavior that are assimilated over time by those who work in the organization. You might have a set of values and attitudes, but you adapt that to the organization itself. Your behavior is shaped by incentives and by how you see others behave, form of self-protection and social control. Organizational culture does not exist in a vacuum within the organization.

It is shaped in part by the broader culture of the society in which it operates. Further, organizational culture is not as monolithic as many assume it to be. There can be subcultures within an organization. For example, IT is one of them with their own mentalities, values and attitudes. Organizational culture may seem to be an intimidating term, and the scope of transforming it may feel impossible, especially when you are not in a leadership role. Transforming culture means changing old beliefs and assumptions that make people behave in a certain way and instilling or embedding new ones. It means changing how people are used to doing things. Because culture is often rooted in emotion, it is easy for people to feel uncomfortable, threatened, or defensive in response to change.

However, it is important to remember that although culture generally resists change, it is also constantly changing. This paradoxical condition limits the speed of change and consumes a large amount of energy. But change is necessary! It is always happening, whether you like it or not. Embracing change and recognizing your individual role as a leader in spearheading it within your organization can ultimately be a rewarding and positive experience, and it is critical to ensuring successful implementation of DevOps. Many organizations have cultures that lean toward traditional ways of doing tasks or outdated ways of thinking that have led to problems like teams working in silos, teams having a defensive and protective instinct toward their own tools and processes, and teams lacking focus on delivering business value and addressing customer needs. A DevOps culture is oriented toward outcomes.

Accordingly, DevOps teams embrace new ideas, work proactively and see problems and failures as learning opportunities. Silos don't exist in a DevOps culture. And team members don't blame individual team members for issues. The team members are mutually accountable and work as a unit. Remember, moving toward a DevOps culture can be challenging for the above reasons. DevOps culture is about sharing responsibility and shifting toward transparency, communication and collaboration across Development and IT Operations and the business.

It emphasizes more multidisciplinary, and cross-functional teams that focus on delivering business value and addressing customer needs. When leaders discuss the kind of culture that supports DevOps, the most important point they discuss and acknowledge is the need for collaboration. Breaking down the wall of confusion and the silos that have caused it requires prioritizing collaboration and teamwork, breaking down the silo mentality that built that wall of confusion in the first place. Collaboration can be a challenge.

As you have learned, organizations are often structured and set up in ways that discourage collaboration. Certain behaviors and attitudes sometimes act as barriers to the kind of collaborations the DevOps demands. These barriers to collaboration must be eliminated to enable a DevOps culture. This task can be difficult because many organizations have barriers in place that actively discourage communication, transparency, trust and accountability. However, without these key characteristics, collaboration becomes impossible and hence, DevOps becomes impossible. Now we will give you some examples of barriers to communication. It can be maybe a long wait time for responses to questions or problems, or maybe inability to request help or ask questions and receive a prompt response. There are some ways to overcome such barriers to communication.

For example, if there are long wait times, then it may be possible to address that barrier with new or better tools for communication, an open office Hmm. Or maybe we can change the seating arrangement or a ticketing system for resolving the problems or issues. Let's look at the barriers to transparency. It may be a lack of understanding about why each team operates in a certain way, or maybe about invisibility of work, which means you cannot see what others are working or having or are doing. There are some ways to overcome such barriers to transparency. For example, if there is a lack of understanding about why each team operates in a certain way, then cross-functional teams could address the barriers or cross team meetings could provide greater transparency.

Let's look for the barriers to trust. Maybe a lack of ability to prioritize each other's needs, or understand each other's challenges. Or maybe, a belief that others do not share priorities or goals. There are some ways to overcome such barriers. For example, a lack of appreciation or recognition of skills could be addressed by introducing new programs that recognize employee achievement or by outlining initiatives through which team members or coaches one another and learn new skills. Let's look for other examples of barriers to accountability.

It can be an overlap of roles and responsibilities which causes conflict or maybe blaming or scapegoating when a project or task fails. There are some ways to overcome such barriers. For example, a lack of feedback from Operations to Development could be addressed by using new or more effective knowledge management systems or tools, or by including a development team member into the Operations team and vice versa.

Sharing and Experimentation

DevOps encourages collaboration and sharing. You have reviewed the acronym CALMS earlier in the Book. The S in CALMS stands for Sharing. Sharing and collaboration are crucial to the successful implementation of DevOps. It is only through collaboration and sharing that DevOps can break through the wall of confusion between Development and Operations. You have learned why Development and Operations need to share priorities and goals to help break down the silos that are currently a problem for IT.

There is also a need for sharing process and knowledge to achieve flow as emphasizing the first way and for sharing feedback as emphasized in the second way. Most importantly, Development and Operations ultimately need to understand that they have always shared successes and failures. Sharing is fundamental to DevOps, therefore DevOps is a collective body of knowledge, formalizing one definition of DevOps or trying to control ideas related to what DevOps is would be antithetical to it. You have reviewed some issues identified as barriers, for example, barriers to communication, transparency, trust and accountability. to the kind of collaboration necessary for adopting DevOps.

Sociologist Ron Westrum classified and categorized, most of those issues as being indicative of a pathological organizational culture. In his model, which was designed to predict safety and performance outcomes in the healthcare industry, he described three types of organizations - pathological, bureaucratic and generative. For our purpose, only pathological and generative cultures have been elaborated further. Pathological cultures are characterized by very low collaboration and cooperation across groups. Information is withheld for personal gain, and blame runs rampant because people are oriented toward power.

Pathological cultures are not safe. This statement means that they create a culture of poor communication and a lack of trust. They lack accountability, and these issues lead to a complete lack of transparency since nobody is comfortable with anyone else knowing what they are doing. Employees working in a pathological culture live in a state of fear - fear of failure, speaking up, being fired or blamed or etc. DevOps requires a generative culture. In generative cultures, information is actively sought; learning and sharing of knowledge are important. Communication is encouraged, and there is true accountability because responsibilities are shared. Nobody fears failure or speaking up, because failure causes enquiry rather than blame.

In addition, new ideas and innovations are not only encouraged, but also implemented. DevOps is about embracing a generative culture. DevOps is also about recognizing that in some cases, the focus could be on introducing new processes, practices and new tools. Remember, culture is not only attitudes. In fact, processes and tools are impacted by culture too. DevOps is about creating a culture in which everyone feels safe and supported.

The culture allows employees to feel empowered and they are able to experiment and innovate. Experimentation is about being able to fail and to recognize that failure is not negative when it results in learning. In fact, when you try new things and embrace new ideas, failure is likely to happen more often, not not less.

In IT, experimentation is usually about proving or disproving hypotheses. This approach will allow you to determine new ways to perform tasks. When you try to determine new ways, though, it is important to have a culture that can handle failure.

DevOps encourages failure, but responsible failure - calculated risks, failing fast in small ways, and then learning and implementing solutions that actually work in the aftermath. To do so, organizations anticipating failure need to be proactive and not reactive toward dealing with failure.

Leadership

Ideally, DevOps should be instituted at a high level, so that it permeates the culture from the top to the bottom. But the reality is that this approach is not always possible. Therefore, a transformational leader, someone who may not necessarily be in a leadership role in an organization, plays an important role. The leader convinces the organization to move in the required direction by maybe establishing and supporting generative and high trust cultural norms. Or by implementing technologies and processes that enable developer productivity, reducing code deployment lead time, and supporting more reliable infrastructures.

By supporting team experimentation and innovation for creating and developing better products at a faster pace. Transformational leaders can also work across organizational silos to achieve strategic alignment. The state of developers reporting 2017 was made by a Puppet Labs measured transformational leadership against these five dimensions that you can see in this chapter. Shifting an organizational culture or even a team or departmental culture toward some generative that reinforces a set of shared priorities and goals and that supports DevOps is in fact a transformation. Transformation requires a vision - a clear, well communicated understanding of why you are seeking to transform and change, and what is the ultimate outcome.

If a vision is developed at the beginning of the DevOps journey, professionals can fall back on it at the future point when they run into questions that demand answers. The vision that will guide them as they move forward. Without a clear vision, an obvious path will not exist when making decisions and implementing new processes or tools. Establishing a vision at the beginning ensures that everything that happens afterward is in alignment. A clear vision also helps professionals to focus more clearly on the results of the transformation and keeps the scope of leadership and change from widening and becoming overwhelming or unclear. To understand transformational leadership further, you need to understand the difference between a traditional leader and a transformational leader. Traditional leadership leans more toward a "command and control" model.

Traditional leaders are more authoritative in nature. They give orders and expect the team to execute those orders. There is not much room for negotiation, discussion or challenge. The style of leadership leads to concentration of knowledge at the top. Think of the phrase on the need-to-know basis. Traditional leaders hoard information, one of the traits you reviewed earlier as being symptomatic of a pathological culture. Transformational leadership encourages flexibility, learning, sharing of knowledge, and most importantly, collaboration. Transformational leadership, which has its basis in Lean leadership, favors facilitation over command and control. Transformational leaders trust that the team members bring their new unique skills and knowledge to the team and prefer to shift the leadership role to someone else. They get the right people together, support them and then get out of their way.

Teams

Harvard Professor Richard Hackman in The Psychology of Self-Management in Organizations outlines levels of team authority that are important when discussing transformational leadership and understanding what a leader's role should be and how DevOps teams should be structured. Review the continuum from traditional manager-led teams to self-organizing and then self-directed teams that Hackman explained in his book.

Understanding these different teams and leadership styles should give you an idea about how transformational leadership for DevOps really needs to be. Manager-led teams. Hackman refers to traditional command-and-control style teams as manager-led teams. In such teams, the manager is responsible for everything, except performing the work. The manager-led style is power oriented, and managers hoard information at the top. This style is not conducive to collaboration. Self managing or self-organizing teams. Hackman refers to self-organizing teams as self-managing teams. Leaders control such teams, design the teams, put them together, and set their overall direction. However, they do not monitor or manage their work processes. They allow team members to have authority over monitoring or managing their work processes.

Self-organizing teams support DevOps. They encourage collaboration and autonomy and destroy silos. The third type is self-directed teams. A level above self-organized teams is self-directed teams. In such teams, leaders are responsible only for setting the overall direction, and the teams themselves are responsible for design and context. Self-directed teams are independent, but the team members are interdependent. Leaders give them a mission and an overall direction, and team members can achieve the mission any way they want. This team model is ideal for Agile and DevOps. Finally, self-governed teams. They are tasked with setting their own overall direction in addition to designing the team structure, managing work processes, and executing tasks. In self organized teams, leaders don't ask only managers to become transformational leaders. Self-organization demands that all team members understand accountability and ownership differently.

To be truly effective, self-organization requires Systems Thinking and understanding of True North and a sense of responsibility for the end to end value stream. You can see the difference between the traditional teams and self organized teams in this chapter. Conway's Law conveys that all designed systems, regardless of the intention, eventually design themselves around the structure of the organization itself. For example, a four layered organizational chart will result in a four-layered approval system. Any new methodology or system you attempt to implement within IT will eventually conform to the existing structure of the IT department and the larger communications structure of the overall organization.

Accordingly, it is very difficult to create a DevOps environment inside of a traditional, vertically structured IT department. That is why the culture stack is so critical. You cannot simply implement DevOps within an existing set of hierarchies and silos, expect that it will be effective, and achieve the desired impact. DevOps requests the right organizational culture and the right leadership to be truly effective. And it also requires the development of self-organized, autonomous teams.

Organizational Structures

We can have a look at different organizational models for DevOps in this chapter. The first type is a vertical structure model. The first attempt at large-scale organization focused on organized vertically. Early tribes organized around a clear leader or group of leaders. That type of organization was adequate for living a relatively peaceful, day-to-day existence, but when we needed to get big tasks accomplished, maybe, for example, attacking other tribes or defending our own, we looked at more military-like structures that were very hierarchical.

Think of the Roman legions in the time before Christ. This structure works well to tame chaotic environments, but it is very reactive and focused on short term goals, leaving the longer term strategic goals to others. The shortcomings of this vertical structure were its inevitable siloed nature. The second type is matrix structure. Next came an offshoot of the vertical structure, the Matrix organization. It was an attempt to overcome the siloed shortcomings of the vertical structure by introducing an additional reporting accountability on a horizontal basis. A given soldier or worker was accountable up the "Chain of Command" and accountable to their coach, mentor, or technology domain leader, thereby making workers "a servant of two masters". What happens when the "two masters" are demanding conflicting priorities? Who wins? In the past, these models seemed to work for IT.

Capacity could be optimized by silo based on demand. Technical knowledge could also be shared throughout the silo hierarchy.

It can be senior practitioners coaching those less experienced. It allowed for career movement, budget accountability and rapid assignment of blame, since if anything goes wrong in a particular technology domain, everyone knows who to blame. There are some weaknesses of the Vertical and Matrix structures that are becoming more and more apparent. Models that operate vertically are less able to manage information from disparate sources such as business applications and users. Each individual business initiative requires involvement across all silos. These structures are slower to respond to business needs when coordination is needed across silos, and numerous handoffs between silos create waste. Product structure is the next stage in the evolution of organization.

In many ways, it is simply a rotation of the vertical structure with all loyalties, measurement or risk, reward, etc, focused around the product. The product structure is all about beating the competition, even within the same company and managing objectives. It is still command and control, but it is more of a meritocracy and rewards, accountability and innovation. It tends to focus on local product oriented optimization. The last one is adaptive structure. It is what DevOps advocates and what the next stage of observable evolution is trending toward. In an adaptive organization, there is a focus on culture, empowerment and employee motivation. It is global optimization over local quick fix. It is about stakeholders, not shareholders, and it works to resemble a family.

The leaders in adaptive organization create a clear vision and mission and then "get out of the way" and let their people figure out how to accomplish it. Adaptive teams are autonomous, self-motivated and self organized. While the term "DevOps Team" is often used, there is a danger related to simply creating another functional silo that sits between Operation and Development. Devops is not necessarily just about creating a specific type of team. Instead, DevOps is a movement for rethinking about teams entirely. It is not simply about creating the one team that "does Devops". Therefore, DevOps is not prescriptive about what a "DevOps Team" should be. Instead, DevOps embraces a variety of patterns and potential structures that enable the right culture, practices and technologies.

The ideal organizational structure that will work for your organization depends upon many variables. Before you review what kind of structure and timing works for DevOps, it is important to understand the myths about DevOps and structures and teaming. Review some of the most common mistakes made when structuring DevOps teams or attempting to implement DevOps. First, there is the DevOps Team Silo. The issue occurs when someone decides that the organization needs DevOps and starts a "DevOps team", without understanding the Full Stack, particularly the cultural changes required to implement DevOps. Without the right culture and leadership, this team simply forms yet another silo, driving Development and Operations even further apart. DevOps doesn't need Operations. Because cloud technology takes care of the needs, Development assumes Operations is outdated, and Development doesn't recognize the importance of Operations' skills and expertise.

This attitude creates further problems between Development and Operations. DevOps as a Tools Team. A DevOps as Tools

Team may be outlined. Accordingly, a team within Development is set up to work on tools related to the deployment pipeline, configuration management and so on. This approach may have benefits, but a DevOps as a Tools Team continues to "throw things over the wall" to Operations, and the fundamental problem of communication and collaboration between Development and Operations continues to remain unresolved.

And the last one is a DevOps engineer. If an organization fails to see IT as business value, they may decide to "do DevOps" and hire a "DevOps engineer" rather than address the gaps in the current culture, processes and technology. This approach represents the System Admin role and simply calls it DevOps. Once again, the fundamental problems remain unresolved. You have learned about some of the most common mistakes made when structuring DevOps or attempting to implement DevOps. Next, review some effective ways to implement structures for DevOps. Increased collaboration between Development and Operations is essential. In the collaborative structure, each team specializes and shares where needed.

Operations as Infrastructure as a Service. In organizations with a very traditional IT Operations department, treating Operations as Infrastructure as a Service might also be an effective way to implement DevOps. This approach involves treating Operations as a team that provides the infrastructure on which applications are deployed and run, and a team within Development as a source of expertise about operation features, metrics, etc. DevOps Team with an expiry date.

It is common to have a DevOps team with an expiry date. This team is created for a specific period, and it aims to bring Development and Operations closer together. This team eventually makes itself obsolete, thus avoiding the problem of the "DevOps team" becoming another silo. With this structure in place, the members of the temporary team act as a bridge and introduce new ideas to each team and help it better integrate with the other. These are just a few of the types of structures and teams that could be considered when implementing DevOps. The dream of DevOps - the ultimate ideal goal - is to evolve teams away from Development and Operations entirely.

The Evolution of Teams

The evolution of DevOps teams takes place in three stages. The first stage of the evolution of a DevOps team structure involves simply introducing changes or new approaches that allow for increased collaboration between development and operations. In this stage, development and operations functions, once siloed, are deployed to create teams that are closely connected and highly collaborative, and that work side by side toward the same goals.

Some organizations take a "you build it, you run it" approach, making developers more responsible for operating their applications in production. This approach helps both teams to understand the needs of each other and further breaks down the silo mentality. The second stage of the evolution of a DevOps team structure involves the formation of a dedicated DevOps team, which is implemented in a way that discourages its existence as another silo. Often, in this stage, the objective is to implement a DevOps Team with the idea of continuing to evolve it in stage three.

According to the 2017 State of DevOps report, only 16 percent of survey respondents in 2014 indicated that they worked on DevOps teams. By 2017 that number increased to 27 percent. The third stage of the evolution of a DevOps team structure involves the reorganization of development and operations to form cross-functional teams. Cross-functional teams are built with representatives of all disciplines who have the responsibility for developing and deploying a service. They are designed to be empowered, self managed, and self-sufficient. These teams may be temporary and assembled only to work on short term projects.

However, they may also be permanent. Most importantly, these teams resemble the adaptive, self-organizing teams. Dysfunctions occur when jobs are designed around tasks or roles. Task orientation leads to silos. It leads to local optimization and discourages Systems Thinking. It also discourages creativity and encourages people to focus only on task execution. Because of the task orientation, jobs become tedious and boring. Further, owing to task orientation, individuals become entrenched in one specialization. Task orientation encourages leaders to micromanage and hoard information. Micromanagement leads to a lack of focus on relationships and innovation.

Moreover, task orientation promotes an attitude of completing your task and not caring about anything else. It also promotes a culture of blaming. To address these problems, leaders need to ensure that they develop cross-functional teams. Leaders consider some important criteria when building cross-functional teams. Leaders balance domain knowledge. A key benefit of a cross-functional team is that it has representatives from different business units or client domains, which are needed to complete the iteration.

Cross-functional teams are designed to include all necessary disciplines. In cross-functional teams, it is important that people with all necessary skills from ideation to implemented iteration are present. The teams should include both functional and non-functional domain expertise. This approach reduces handoffs and the need for detailed documentation. Leaders balance technical skills levels based on a team size. There is a mix of senior and junior type roles to support mentoring, development and the assignment of appropriate work. Leaders also seek diversity. Diversity can mean many different things - gender, race and culture beyond just three among them.

Perhaps, equally important can be how individuals think about problems, how they make decisions, how much information they need before making a decision, and so on. Leaders also consider persistence as important. It takes time to form and develop highly efficient teams. Therefore, they acknowledge the need to keep team members who have worked well together in the same group as much as possible. Now, review is a difference between generalists and pure specialists, and the way a DevOps team needs to balance the two, Building a cross-functional team can be a challenge because it requires a level of practical specialization. Generalists may not have adequate knowledge or skills related to specific tasks or requirements, whereas pure specialists might have difficulty being asked to work outside of their specialization and accept new challenges.

DevOps teams work best when they are created around products or platforms versus specific functions. Product and platform teams require cross-functional skills. They demand more from each individual, but they allow people to dedicate themselves to fewer projects and see them through to completion, or to be responsible throughout the entire lifecycle. Product and platform teams further reduce handoffs, encourage feedback, and motivate and inspire team members by granting them autonomy and recognizing the broad skill sets. They address the problems of task orientation. Let's review the basic structure of DevOps product and platform teams here. You will understand the structure in more detail later.

For your initial analysis, here is an example of a DevOps product and platform team structure. At the top, you have the customers who now interact directly with what used to be development - the product teams who now own products throughout their lifecycle. They are focused on delivering business value through the delivery of software. The product teams develop, run and maintain their application using platform services that are delivered by what used to be operations. The platform teams and the product teams continue to be responsible for maintenance of their application in production.

The platform teams are not responsible for the applications. They are responsible only for providing the platform services. All environments used by the product teams represent production environments for the platform teams. The customers of the platform teams are the product teams. They are expected to support and assist the product teams.

The product teams interact with the end users, that is customers. This approach is the ultimate evolution of teaming in DevOps, and it enables continuous delivery and provides the optimal balance between speed and agility required by the business. This concept is only achievable when you truly understand the Full Stack - the way it integrates people and culture, processes and practices ,and technology and automation.

Book Structure

In this chapter, you will further understand the benefits of automation and the tools for a DevOps toolchain. You will learn about Continuous Integration, Automated Build, Automated Testing, Automated Provisioning, Automated Deployment, cloud technology and virtualization, and architecture for Continuous Delivery.

At the end of this chapter, you will be able to list the ways in which DevOps transforms and organizes technology through automation and new tools to solve the technological problems facing IT.

Development Pipeline

We've already covered that DevOps is not an automation. But it is very important to automate most of the steps in the deployment pipeline. We have covered the Three Ways before. Now, I just want you to remind them. The First Way of automation is to create flow. The Second Way is to ensure that feedback is given consistently. And The Third Way is to allow for experimentation and learning. This quote by Bill Gates conveys that automating bad processes will result in bad results.

It is meant to reinforce the idea that a solid foundation of culture and processes are more important than tools and automation. Before you decide to automate, you should plan to do it in a strategic way. First, use Lean practices to closely examine the process you wish to automate and identify where the waste is, where the constraints are, and what are the high value parts of the process. Then you can automate the high value and repetitive tasks. Automate in a way that optimizes workflow, reduces bottlenecks and facilitates communication among teams. Improve feedback by implementing automated monitoring and modification. Remember, automating bad processes will result in bad results.

Therefore, you learned about the culture and practices layers of the Full Stack first. And now you are learning to apply technology and automation to the processes and practices. Automation is critical to DevOps because it is a primary way that IT can meet the challenges of both agility, speed and innovation on the one hand and maturity, risk and compliance on the other. Automation eliminates waste by removing human labor from the processes where it is not needed, and by minimizing handoffs and rework. It allows for faster recovery when failure occurs by standardizing and reducing variability in processes and making it easier to identify and correct errors and avoid passing them downstream. It removes constraints and creates flow, speeding processes up.

In addition, it ensures that processes are repeatable, again eliminating rework. These benefits help IT move faster. Automation also ensures that processes are measurable, which means that reports can be generated more quickly, and more data can be obtained to improve processes, ensure stability, and mitigate the risk. You will now learn how the concept of automation lines up with the development pipeline and the concept of a toolchain. DevOps automates processes by creating a toolchain, which is made of integrated and complementary tools, often from different vendors, that provide the capabilities required to automate each stage of the deployment pipeline. Each stage of the pipeline provides a new opportunity to verify the quality of features and provide feedback.

A toolchain provides transparency and visibility related to the flow of changes and work. An effective DevOps toolchain reinforces collaboration and avoids silo mentality. The table lists examples of tools commonly used in different stages of the deployment pipeline. Generally, many tools cross over and overlap between various stages of the pipeline. This indicates that by adopting DevOps, organizations become committed to breaking down silos. Tools such as Slack or Trello are used to increase communication and collaboration. Further, tools such as New Relic are used to monitor and alert.

DevOps does not recommend any specific toolset. Organizations or teams can examine and explore the available tools to identify the ones that work for them. You just learned about some tools used for each stage of the deployment pipeline in a DevOps toolchain. Additionally, a variety of different elements and tools are used within a DevOps toolchain. Not all of them automate the deployment pipeline and continuous delivery. Some support DevOps through automating other important tasks and processes, which you can see in the chapter. In this chapter, we will look at five stages of DevOps automation of deployment pipelines. They are continuous integration, automated build, automated testing, automated provisioning and automated deployment.

We will look at each of them shortly in the next chapters. Continuous integration is about automating the process through which developer-working copies are merged into a shared code repository or main code trunk. Automated Build involves automating the process of taking the committed code in the source repository and automatically compiling it into a package ready for validation and deployment. Automated Testing includes testing through an automated tool across the pipeline to increase feedback and to correct defects.

Automated provisioning involves taking the outputs of the Automated build after they have gone through the appropriate automated tests and then assembling them into an Automated Platform as a Service that is ready for deployment. Automated deployment uses Application Feature toggles that hide features from the customer even when code is already deployed into the production environment, but allow for internal or customer segment testing to occur.

Cloud Technology

Cloud has changed everything. Over the years, more and more third party services have emerged to handle the traditional work of IT departments. Service automation has allowed companies to further minimize or reduce the manual processes previously handled by IT to increase efficiency and profit margins. IT is no longer a differentiator. Startups now have the ability to immediately utilize cloud services to put an IT infrastructure in place and get it up and running. Therefore, it is worth knowing how the cloud has transformed the world and IT. Cloud computing is defined by five key characteristics.

On-demand self-service means with a cloud service, users can provision resources and capabilities like server time and network storage automatically without the need for human interaction. They may use a self-service portal or management console based on the web. Broad network access means resources are accessible via a network and through standard mechanisms, including a variety of mobile devices and workspaces that might be required by the users. Resource pooling means a cloud service can be available to multiple customers using the same physical resources. This is known as the multi-tenant model, which is achieved by assigning and reassigning resources dynamically according to user demand. Rapid elasticity means resources are provisioned and released with the ability to quickly scale outward and inward based upon user demand.

Measured service means resource usage is controlled and optimized by leveraging an appropriate metering capability.

Usage is then monitored, measured and built according to utilization. It is pay for use. Cloud computing is about utilizing technology as a service. Cloud technology contributes to the creation of new efficiencies and new processes that enable automation and make IT better, faster, and cheaper than ever before. Therefore, by adopting DevOps and utilizing cloud technology and automation, businesses can plan and implement Continuous Delivery and gain a strategic advantage over their competition. Many large companies provide public cloud services with the most established being Amazon Web services, launched in 2006.

Rackspace began offering cloud computing with Mosso in 2008. It took until 2010 for major names like IBM and Microsoft to finally launch their offerings, with Dell following them in 2011. Google and HP only entered the Public cloud sphere in 2012. Public cloud computing is relatively new, but it is quickly becoming a necessity and the critical tool of IT. Public is the most prevalent of the three common deployment models for cloud computing, where commercial cloud services can be used by and available to anyone through virtualization. A good example of public is Amazon Web services. It provides reliable and inexpensive cloud computing that is location independent. Private is not exposed to the public, and it resides behind the firewall and within a single organization, allowing only that organization to access and manage it. It can be more expensive, but offers security, flexibility and greater control than the public option.

Hybrid describes cloud services that exist both publicly and privately, with those applications that require security and privacy in a certain organization's network, while other services are hosted using a public cloud. This option may not be visible to the end users, and it will be considered interchangeable in day to day operations and more cost effective than the private cloud, while also allowing for the security of the private option. Here you can see the difference between different types of cloud services. In the traditional on premise cloud services, we manage everything from networking, storage, servers, virtualization and apps. In the infrastructure as a service model, we don't manage the hardware side, we start managing from the operating system and upwards to the applications.

In the platform as a service model, we only manage the data and applications, other things managed by the provider. And in the Software as a Service, the provider manages everything. We can only make some changes in settings and small changes to the software. You just learned four service models for cloud computing: traditional on premise cloud services, infrastructure as a service, platform as a service. and software as a service. As businesses move from having full control with a traditional on premises cloud service toward software as a service, they achieve more standardization, and they lower the costs. They also get faster time to value. Software as a service offers a quick start, and it can be managed with minimal ongoing effort. However, the more they move toward software as a service, the less customization is available to them.

And out of the box software as a service option will not be built for their specific needs. It will instead be more standard with less fixed flexibility. While these four cloud computing models are crucial for you to understand the evolution of DevOps, they are not the only service models that exist. There are many examples of those four models being tweaked to outsource or manage other specific components of the cloud. This is known as Everything as a service. Varieties of options are available, and they can support or complement DevOps and will continue to evolve as we move forward. Earlier, you reviewed one of the critical ways in which Everything as a Service supports DevOps practices such as configuration and release management through another concept, that is, everything as a code or software defined everything.

Increasingly, software is defining everything. Everything is easy becoming code, virtualized, or abstract, as opposed to being physical. This development allows for increased flexibility, connectivity and speed of service. As software defined everything, then everything is stored in the cloud. This development offers new possibilities for IT and enables the balance of speed and reliability that is represented by DevOps.

Architecting for Continuous Delivery

DevOps teams work best when architected around products or platforms versus basic functions. One of the requirements of evolution to product and platform teams is decoupled architecture. Decoupled. architecture was employed to build the Spotify app in which the app's features and functions could be used and improved independently while still interfacing with each other. This approach allowed Spotify to have different teams or squads, each responsible for different aspects of the product and a different client platform.

Decoupled architecture is accomplished through microservices. Containers are a solution to the problem of how to get software to run reliably when moved from one computing environment to another. This movement could be from a developer's laptop to a test environment, from a staging environment into production, and perhaps, from a physical machine in a data center to a virtual machine in a private or public cloud. Each container has a complete runtime environment for the specific service or application. Each computing environment simply has to run the container.

A container consists of an entire runtime environment: an application, its dependencies, libraries and other binaries, and configuration files needed to run it, which are bundled into one package. By containerizing the application platform and its dependencies, differences in OS distributions and underlying infrastructure are abstracted away. Containerization is different from virtualization, because virtualization technology, the package that can be passed around is a virtual machine, and it includes an entire operating system as well as application. A physical server running three virtual machines would have a hypervisor and three separate operating systems running on top of it.

By contrast, a server running three containerized applications as with Docker runs a single operating system, and each container shares the operating system kernel with the other containers. Shared parts of the operating system are read only, while each container has its own mount for writing. That means the containers are much more lightweight and use far fewer resources than virtual machines. Microservice architecture is a software development technique that structures an application as a collection of loosely coupled services that talk to each other through a separate communication layer. In the microservice architecture, services are fine grained and the protocols are lightweight.

You will now review the difference between service oriented architecture and microservice architecture. Service oriented architecture separates functions into distinct units or services, which developers make accessible over a network to allow users to combine and reuse them in the production of applications. These services and their corresponding consumers communicate with each other by passing data in a well defined shared format, or by coordinating an activity between two or more services. Microservice architecture is a variant of the service oriented architecture architectural style. Applications are structured as a collection of loosely coupled services. This approach makes applications much more flexible and easier to understand, develop, and test.

And, most importantly, it enables teams to develop, deploy and scale services independently. Microsphere's architecture makes Continuous Delivery and Continuous Deployment possible. Microservice are great, but most existing applications are not designed to accept the addition of new models. Further, for many businesses, shutting down large monolithic applications to recreate them as microservices is logistically impossible. So, what can you do if you have a monolithic legacy application that you want to replace with microservices? What you can do over time is to slowly, iteratively introduce microservices that are able to seamlessly replace specific features and functions.

The process should be designed to replace one function at a time. If done correctly, this process will be transparent to the end user. A dispatcher is added to ensure that customers are sent to the correct location, to microservice or to monolithic application, for each requested function until, finally, the monolithic application is entirely replaced over time, having been effectively "strangled" by all the smaller microservices. The dispatcher remains to route customer requests to the correct microservice. This phenomenon of many smaller apps slowly taking over the tasks of the larger app is called the Strangler Application Pattern.

Notice the difference between Strangler application and Strangler application pattern. The overtaking microservice is a Strangler application. The approach of gradually replacing a monolithic application with microservices over time is the Strangler application pattern. Thank you for completing this

Book. If you have any questions, please feel free to contact me. I really hope you found this Book valuable, but either way, please leave a review and share your experience. Have a nice day!